T0380907

I Know the Feeling

Spider Ward Pumfrey

To order additional copies of this book, contact:
Xlibris
AU TFN: 1 800 844 927 (Toll Free inside Australia)
AU Local: 0283 108 187 (+61 2 8310 8187 from outside Australia)
www.xlibris.com.au
Orders@Xlibris.com.au

ISBN: Softcover   978-1-7960-0833-3
        Hardcover   978-1-7960-0835-7
        EBook   978-1-7960-0834-0

Library of Congress Control Number: 2019919640

Print information available on the last page

Rev. date: 11/03/2020

"I Know The Feeling"

The Cover and the Artist

I would like to thank Spider Ward-Pumfrey for choosing this beautiful artwork of Arch Angel Raphael, the Healer. I am SueRose, the artist. I have been painting since I was young. And seeing Angels since I was aged four. I have this amazing connection with these beautiful beings. Now I am selling my Spiritual Art all over the world and sharing my gift.

Blessings,

SueRose

maitlandmagpie@hotmail.com

This little book is dedicated to my darling husband Michael and you the reader. With love to the moon and back.

Contents

Acknowledgements

The miracle question has to be, what would I change in my life from the past and today the answer would have to be, nothing. Finally, not always gently, the pieces of the puzzle have fallen into place and I am profoundly grateful and humbled by my amazing journey so far. I have some truly amazing friends and chosen family and blood kin. I am privileged on so many different levels and I think all of my teachers, Angels I didn't recognise, and all of the lessons for empowering me to change perspective. The beautiful Angel TraShell, Founder at Royal Psychic Live TV and International Psychic Medium, always believed I would write my book. We all have colleagues and sometimes those colleagues become exceptional friends and members of our chosen soul family. When I asked Elizabeth Van Den Broek who would help me publish my book, it was Elizabeth who quietly wrote the answer in lower case so I could read it and that's how I found my Publisher.

Finally, it is with unconditional love and humble thanks to my darling friend Rita-Marie Lenton. (She is my go-to, when I can't find things, in our new home in Queensland). Rita-Marie calmly led me to Paula, from Beyond the Maize, who promptly answered my hysterical email and brought the beautiful scribe Benjerlee to my door. Without these wonderful earth Angels, including Tracey Stranger, patiently inserting final editing, this book would never have made it to my amazing publishers, Xlibris.

Plus, One of my favourite places is Buddhas Essence of Healing, 13A Sydney Crescent, Lalor 3075, Melbourne, Australia and the very beautiful owner Alex Morgan Psychic Medium.

info@alexmorgan.com.au

Foreword

Thank you for picking up this book. We live in an animated world ruled by technology and machines designed to help us move forward to a better freer life.

Some of us are "called to be of service" we just have to help. We are for the most part kind and compassionate to the point of subservient.

As the new age battles mainstream religion, both claiming to be right, it is my hope that this book guides you to taking what's good for you from both sides of the fence.

I have tried to stay in one or the other. It simply did not sustain me. The more I learned the more alike the two were and I began to pick what worked in my belief system – inclusiveness.

In answer to a prayer, I found they were in essence both right, and that I was able to combine elements from everywhere that empowered me to have a better relationship with my Heavenly Father and his Son. The stronger my faith became the wider my focus became.

The result is this little book. Words not carved in granite, but words that open the possibility for something better.

Encaustic art is a joyous tool for clairsentient people. It allows for connection to meditate and for self. I have always found that creating art has a calming effect. It allows me to express my awareness of now ("without judgement") it is not about the end product. It is also not new. It is more about your feelings and attitude when you begin. If you believe, as I do, that the divine is in everything, then what is produced is truly beautiful as I am always humbled by the process.

The encaustic (wax) art presented here in this book is for you to look at and explore what you feel and what you can use as you continue to look.

It is created using heated beeswax which I have pigmented colours added at the time of heating.

This can then be used to create the desired effects. It has lots of layers or just a few. It is quite mesmerising to look at (according to records, the genre was perfected by Pausias, a Greek painter in the 4th century BC).

I have endeavoured to share with you encaustic works using only one colour so that you can perhaps try. For example, the "blue flow" page could be used for feelings involving the throat chakra and blockages – "Not speaking your truth".

Then again you may just like it because it is blue! No hard and fast rules "I just know the feeling".

The Beginning

This book is purpose built so it won't be for everyone. We all try to be the drum major of our own band and yet sometimes we still feel like a "square peg in a round whole". And we long to fit.

My purpose therefore, is to act as a guide, an explanation for the "feeling people" those who get overwhelmed by emotions or in other words, swamped by energies.

As we approach 2021, balanced mental health and wellbeing has become very, very, important to each and every one of us. Simply put, this is the state of being comfortable in our own skin, healthy and happy "with social stability" and peace. I take this to include "morals, upbringing, empathy, adaptability, social circumstances".

I feel the feelings. I have learnt not to become the emotion. I can be a witness. Process, and set it free.

I would now like to share a list of some of the things that used to happen to me when I was a much younger and confused teenager this continued for much of my adult life.

Take a deep breath and read very fast with me:

Anxiety, panic attacks, seriously hypersensitive to noise, making a meal out of precious fingernails, cancelling things you said yes to right at the very last minute. Being overstimulated and frightened in busy places (like big shopping malls), and unwarranted, emotional, explosive outbursts that don't fit the situation and can be quite out of control. Now if all this isn't enough, there is the spooky world of thinking, over thinking and rethinking and of course I can't leave out the fact that you can't calm down and that causes chest pain and then you feel like it's a heart attack. What a roller coaster!! BREATHE AGAIN.

We are called clairsentient, clear feelers "I feel therefore I know" (Spiderism). For example, when you get sick you go to the doctor, he tells you what's wrong and then he tells you how to treat/manage the illness to recover (over simplified I know). The point being, you have been informed, and you now have a choice to follow the advice or not.

And so it is with clairsentience, it is a gift – which you can use to enhance the quality of life, put fears that you are "barking mad", finally to rest and hopefully improve the quality of relationships with people in your life.

I hate writing, primarily because I am dyslexic and adding to my existing woes in life was the struggle to spell.

I am always mindful that if I write, particularly about myself, that I am writing my own indictment for the Spanish Inquisition. I have been the whipping boy, not always as a volunteer, and it took many years to understand that my being different had a purpose not designed to destroy me. I was always the different kid, I was the kid that knew stuff (scary spooky stuff) so I was already guilty just for standing in the room and overwhelmed constantly by the normal emotions that run in any family.

Clairsentience means clear, true, unjustifiable "knowing". It is the amazing ability to move across a time and stay in that time and be consciously aware of all feeling in any given space. That knowledge becomes a double edged sword because it is exact and connects the old world with the immediate present world as far back as the Akashic Record (that's everything that occurred in the past the present or the future and they're encoded in an etheric way of all human events, thoughts and words).

Empaths, according to the oxford dictionary, is a person with the ability to perceive the mental or emotional state of another individual. Often times a true empath is capable of taking on the pain of others at their own expense (https://psychalive.org>emp).

Clairsentience/Empaths are usually old souls and old souls have been around forever. Likewise the urban dictionary suggests "originates from a nursery rhyme Old King Cole was a merry old soul" (a person who is wise upon their years: people of strong emotional stability, basically, someone who has more understanding of the world around them. And the nursery rhyme comes from 1708. We often look at new born babies and their eyes are intense when they look at you and even people that are not spiritually inclined recognise the intense stare of an old soul. Words often associated with old souls are that they bring peace, truth, knowledge and wisdom. They have incredibly strong bonds with the ancient ones. Should you find that you fit a clairsentient/empath who just happens to be an old soul as well then it takes a long time to grow into the mould? The younger years are frustrating because you are older than the children you are attending school with. There is also, from the day you are born, an unbelievable sense of being responsible for everything and everyone and their wellbeing.

An intuitive (clairsentient) is a person who senses energy everywhere. People, surroundings, objects and this intense experience is not evident to all people. This clear feeling (intuition) is really strong. For example, ordinary folk know the difference between hot and cold, intuitive people, who we can also call psychic, know it is going to get cold, it is going to get hot, it is going to rain because they feel it coming. To further complicate these feelings is an empathetic ability which is common to many intuitive people, so they also know/sense what the people around them are feeling and thinking and sometimes going to do (the serious spooky part of these words is that clairsentient empaths know when you are lying so it's a waste of time, not even worth putting to the test). We who are clairsentient empaths have minds which are highly attuned to the vibrational frequency by those around them. This information is then refined into instinctively knowing what to do in any situation.

Could you be a Clairsentient/Empath?

1. **You are curious by things that are ancient and you understand historical timelines.**
   Deep in your soul, since you were little, there has been a sense that you are not from this time (ET phone home) and there is a sadness attached to this because you know you can never go home and so you seek comfort in the ancient world.

2. **You have a magical ability to empathise.**
   So when someone is sad, you know exactly what sad feels like, you know what lost feels like, you know what angry feels like, you know what unwanted feels like, the list is endless.

3. **Your inner circle is very small.**
   There is only so much energy and feeling a clairsentient empath can cope with on any given day. If their energy level at the football, when a goal is scored, is 10 (as high as it can get) and a riot with protesters is also energy 10, then it is neither good or bad for you, it's just overwhelming, so we probably won't find you dancing in the mosh pit.

4. **You are not found in dark places.**
   We are afraid of the dark because we feel we need the light on to see where we are going.

5. **You get lost in clutter.**
   Ambiance is incredibly important we are comforted by nice.

6. **Cruelty to animals**
   We cannot cope with mean and uncaring people. Particularly where our fur babies are concerned.

7. **Sometimes you can be overwhelmed by energies you feel in new places.**
   A party where you don't know anyone, new school, new job, new people.

8. **You are quick to understand root problems.**
9. **You are very sensitive to your feelings.**
10. **You are overwhelmed by loud noises.**
11. **You can be affected by other people's negative eg. travelling on public transport.**
12. **You can be overwhelmed by intense emotions of happiness, sadness, anger, grief and loss.**
13. **You have monumental trust issues.**
14. **You are called to be of service to others.**
    This is divine purpose, to help humanity is our job, so claircentient folk are often found in helping professions eg. nursing, rehabilitation, teaching etc.

15. **You are not very good at saying NO!!!!!!**
    "Blessed are the peace makers" because angry outbursts overwhelm us we find clever, logical and

practical ways to keep the peace, and if that included saying no then we can't do it. No will cause trouble, no will get us hurt, no will create a nightmare that we can't fix.

16. **You can feel the presence of others.** It is important to remember that for the most part, an empath feels emotions and a clairsentient person has the ability to use all senses of smell, hear, sight (not always clearly). The sense of smell is heightened in people who are intuitive, so some clairsentient people will choose to detach from the empath and their soul in order to fit in. So clairsentient people have a physical response, whereas, empaths just feel the emotions. It is worthy to note, that clairsentient people are natural researchers who have trust issues, so feel free to test me out and have a wander through google using any of the words that we have used. Then what you have is a validation, and then you can decide to trust me or not.

Is this you? Some or all? Is this helping?

_____

_____

_____

_____

_____

_____

_____

_____

_____

_____

_____

_____

_____

_____

_____

_____

_____

_____

_____

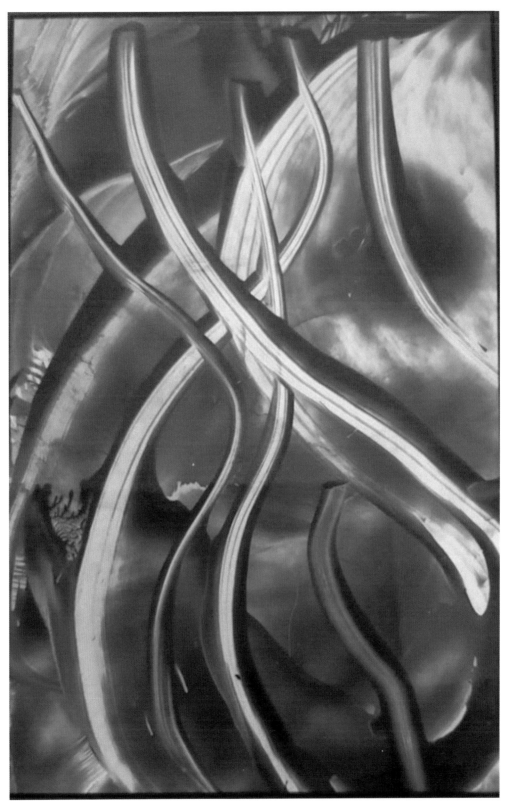

The Blue Flow, (Encaustic Wax Art) original by Spider Ward, 2014

What is happening as you read is that you are becoming more self-aware. This leads to a competence which leads to better skills and management. In short you become grounded.

This grounding allows you to then explore rationally how you problem solve which may lead to a better understanding of you. As ambiguous as that may seem, it is about what we do with what we know. "For every action (force) in nature there is an equal and opposite reaction" (Newton's Laws of Motion – NASA https://www.grc.nasa.gov.newton).

As we become more aware of whom we are, we begin to attract "different". This "different" sometimes includes new friends, old friends, moving further away, new interests and a slow realisation that we are not so weird after all. That we are unique and we belong.

"Se necesita unpueblo criar a un nino" (Carlos) translates to, "It takes a village to raise a child".

This could be the motto of the clairsentient club – We simply don't like to be alone in our endeavours – we need to be "part of". Sadly, we will sacrifice who we are to be part of things we don't agree with and people we don't necessarily like. So strong is the need to belong.

To be clairsentient is to be a member of a huge tribe of caring compassionate souls and the most I feel underrated and misunderstood. This makes us incredibly vulnerable to thoughtlessness and jealousies. In a world that is over qualified, people who instinctively know, without academic qualification, are often discarded and disrespected.

The good news in this gloom is that we are the fixers, the go to when the world collapses around others. The others know we will always answer the call for help and instinctively know how to bring calm, kindness and solution.

The curse of clairsentient is how quickly you feel drained. It's like somebody left the hose on and emptied your tanks. Sometimes it manifests as just feeling lightheaded. Sometimes it manifests as goose bumps. Goose bumps can also be a validation for you that your clear feeling is true and you nailed it. It can also be a sign to run away, like being overwhelmed by the crowd, as in a Westfield Shopping Centre. There can also be a sense of foreboding that violence has occurred. You can get stressed out by the never ending stream of emotions that you feel and this can lead to feeling anxious, depressed, and even suicidal. So once you understand the gift, you then learn how to manage it and not put your physical self in jeopardy. Sometimes we choose to shut this down because it's too hard, and we learn to pretend that we are something that we are not with disastrous consequences and people become really introverted and afraid and stay in a permanent state of nothingness. This takes a great deal of energy and is often the reason why we feel tired all the time.

As clairsentients we listen and answer to a higher self and we know the most appropriate course of action at any particular moment, while remaining acutely aware of feelings.

Two of the hardest life lessons the clairsentient person must learn as early as possible is to be discerning and to be detached and most clairsentient people would rather not learn either. The challenge is how to stay grounded. So that we can remain fully in the present and not get caught up in circumstances which are primarily none of our business.

The second lesson is a true challenge to the heart of the clairsentient soul, detachment. Detachment is the state of being objective in a rather unemotional way. It is to choose to be separated from the person, place or thing. In other words, you are choosing not to be personally involved.

When we deal with "now" and don't get lost in "what if".

Stay in the Moment

The practice of staying present will heal you.
Obsessing about how the future will turn out creates anxiety.
Replaying broken scenarios from the past causes
anger or sadness.
Stay here, in this moment.

– S. McNutt

We acknowledge the trauma of the past, we can centre our minds entirely on the present, and we are remarkably resilient and optimistic souls. We are very likeable people. People sense that we can be trusted, and we bring calm to chaos. We are creative, imaginative and when we make time for peaceful relaxation we do not get overwhelmed.

My plan as we work through the book together is that you begin to get a sense of community and that we are there for one another. Clairsentient anxiety is like a double dose of regular anxiety because it is almost impossible to turn off the absorption. So technically speaking what works for one works for the other. I am a big fan of problem solving with chocolate if you can believe it, doing a domestic chore, anything from folding clothes to washing dishes, hug a tree, take your shoes off, feel the earth beneath your feet, put yourself in your pink bubble, explore the virtues of lavender and bergamot. Herb tea's like chamomile can be soothing, candles and aromatherapy, what a joy! It is empowering to work out your triggers, what sets it off. Have you picked up someone else's fear? Or are you frightened? There is great calm in routine, and of course, using compassionate mindful strategies all help to bring us back to our grounded centre and you very quickly learn what doesn't work. Believe me… I know the feeling.

I See the Moon and the Moon Sees Me

Clairsentients/Empaths are interchangeable names. You can be both or just one and this is why often times the job description, if taken literally, does not fit. However, when you take into account how balanced your life "isn't" at the moment, it is reasonable to assume it is because you are out of step with your ruling planet the moon, often referred to as "She" (The Goddess).

A little bit of trivia, the metal gold is masculine and associated with the sun and the metal silver is associated with the feminine (The moon).

If you are inclined to work with Angels, as I delight in doing, then the Arch Angel is Haniel. The precious stone is moonstone, the planet is Venus and should you evoke this Angel then you are doing so "for the getting of wisdom".

It is interesting to note that the clairsentient person can be quiet happy on a blue-sky day at the beach. However, if the wind comes up and the waves become too big, too loud and too sandy then the clairsentient person has no choice to go home and try and recover from the shock. A better place to spend the day is by bay water, lake, dam, babbling brook. As in the immortal words of the 23rd psalm, "he leads me by still water". We quite like parks and fountains and generally don't go anywhere where there isn't plumbing. The term lunar alignment for me has always been time to down tools, regroup and replenish. Permission to rest.

Lunar alignment for sentient souls is a "God given gift" simply because we may not be able to refuse the calls for help. However, come the full moon, that's our RDO (Rostered Day Off) or night off. It is the art of just being enveloped in a glorious night of precious little effort. Nurturing the human-self with mindful kindness. This is not easy for the clairsentient person to do, or give permission, to take the night off and so it must be a discipline learnt. It must be a boundary on the night of the full moon. The only client, child, wife, sister, husband drama on the table is yours. This can be done in a couple of ways. Me, I take the easy road, stay home, eat comfort food, macaroni and cheese, Tim Tam's and ice cream, soak in a tub, light candles, watch a movie with a happy ending or just simply chill. You might like to try meditation, yoga, some kind of creativity. Whatever you choose, it must be conducive to your wellbeing and happiness.

This quiet time, "the night of a full moon", is a home night to bond with self and soul. The time for the core of self only. This is my version of lunar alignment. It is for the soul's purpose of centring in the here and now. Conscious awareness, replenishing batteries, with no real demands on physical sense and I am quite literally, not available to the outside world until the next day.

As a clairsentience/claircognicent psychic councillor, I found it was imperative to be simple in my down time and it had to be consistent with simple pleasures and comforts. The restoration of hope in one easy lesson each month, only having to manage the "call to be of service" to each full moon replenish, and begin again in the new moon. This takes approximately 3 full moons to create a habit. You may not notice a lot of change with the first moon however, by the second moon you are starting to get a feel for the cycle you are creating and come the third moon all is how it should be – balanced (and you won't double book, you won't give it away because it is your life line).

Because we feel, we are ruled by energies (wind, rain, fire, pestilence, relatives, motherhood/fatherhood and starvation). We can be in a constant state of feeling drained and incompetent, a total "sooky la la" (a recognised Aussie phrase meaning an overly emotional or sensitive person, who gets upset like a small child).

The clairsentient soul needs to understand its boundaries. Once set in place these boundaries help produce appropriate solutions.

The Arch Angel Raphael (on the cover) and the Arch Angel Zadkiel are two amazing Angels to work with (you do not have to work with Angels; you can try all of these ideas in your own time and space. I know it works better with Angels).

Arch Angel Raphael is commonly known for healing and he is mentioned in the Old Hebrew Bible in the Book of Tobit and Raphael means, "god heals" or in Hebrew it means, "he who heals". Often times he is seen with Mother Mary. The colour frequency is green (malachite).

Arch Angel Zadkiel is the righteousness of God (according to Wikipedia), Arch Angel of freedom, benevolence, mercy and memory and the colour frequency is violet.

I like to also include an Ascended Master (Ascended Masters are believed to be spiritually enlightened beings who in past incarnations were ordinary humans, but who have undergone a series of spiritual transformations: Wikipedia)

For clairsentient people, the truly beautiful and gifted St Germaine representing forgiveness, mercy and soul freedom. Please don't think that these are the only Angels and he is the only master. We each have Angels close to our heart, and masters who guide and teach us and you can choose to work with anyone at any time, for the purpose of understanding who you are as a clairsentient soul in a modern world. This little book is probably a very good cheat sheet to get you started on your own understanding of who you are.

How are you feeling now?

If you have gotten this far and you are feeling like finally someone understands, then it's time for you to do a little work. What are you feeling, what has fallen into place and what questions are running through your mind?

_____

_____

_____

_____

_____

_____

_____

_____

_____

_____

_____

_____

_____

_____

_____

_____

_____

_____

_____

_____

_____

_____

"The Healing Heart" (Encaustic Wax Art) original by Spider Ward, 2014

The easiest way to put clarity and perspective on psychic gifts is to give you a choice.

Clairsentients is "clear feeling, receiving guidance and information through your body and your feelings" **Claircognizance** is "clear thinking", receiving guidance and information through your thought, knowing what is a truth and right.

Clairvoyance is "clear seeing", receiving guidance and information through your physical sight, third eye ("mind's eye").

Clairaudience is "clear hearing", receiving guidance and information through auditory means, physically hearing or in your spiritual ear (as when God called Samuel).

And so the shift has begun and you are beginning to realise you can feel you are a more knowing person than you used to be. The thing that is about to change, is we now find intolerable those things we use to accept and tolerate. This doesn't mean that you have suddenly morphed into a "Spider-Warrior", however, the battlefield has changed, and your new weapon is silence. The old you argued for the truth and what has changed is you are selective in how you disperse your time, your focus and your energies.

Example: A Clairvoyant person sees the hole in the ground ahead and goes "there is a hole" and they walk around it. The clairsentient person says "I feel the tension", I know something is wrong, danger ahead and falls in the hole. After a few sooky la' la' moments, the truly remarkable transcendent soul find its way out of the hole. Three weeks later, the sentient person, again walking in the same place, hears a cry for help, follows the voice, sees another person has fallen in the hole, and jump in the hole. The person in the hole says "well that's just wonderful", now we are both stuck here and the transcendent soul says "yes, but I'm going to show you the way out". This is the strength, frailty and magnificence of the clairsentient soul. In this chapter we are going to explore the importance of protection and care for your physical energetic body so that you stay strong and healthy (Spiderward).

Clairsentient people have an in-built radar and generally are smart enough not to eat stuff that they know for certain will make them sick. Usually the sensation is it might be "icky". It is no more professional than that because of your own natural ability to discern whether or not you are comfortable, then you have an ability to decide what you put in your mouth. Clairsentient people often benefit from the one day fast and because we like food too much, it's not going to last much longer than that! I have started at breakfast and the fast was over by 10 o'clock.

Clairsentient people by nature are also very sensitive to smells and taste. Throw in feelings, not liking loud noises, and being overwhelmed by emotions, than it is reasonable to assume that extremes in foods and beverages can have a drastic effect, regardless of what the smell is. If it's too intense, than our sensitive soul is immediately overwhelmed. Panic sets in, fear jumps into the driver's seat, panic attack goes from standby to full activation in a public place then we have a lost, overwhelmed, freighted little person. There are a few rules that seem to work and that is advanced planning at home, for the most part, you control the vibration, if you have to go out then don't place yourself in a situation where you can be overwhelmed. If life in the fast lane has bogged me down, and I have to go to the pub for dinner, then my husband Michael already knows, he will say "what would you like" and I reply "whatever you get me will be perfect" this translates to rump steak, medium well, mushroom sauce, salad and chips. I know what it is, I know I like it, and I know I will eat it when it is put in front of me (get out of jail free card). The reason I have shared this with you is that I am solution based in everything I do. This is how I have learnt to manage my psychic gift. This world of ours is where I live, it's where my friends are, it's where my clients are and I have to be able to walk out my front door, and love my life with purpose, happiness and joy. That might sound a little pie in the sky "dolly do good" but all of the clairsentient signs, like the goose bumps, like the dry throat and the heightened senses and awareness have a place. Not on standby 24/7, 365 days per year, 24 hours a day.

In order to be of service and do my job, if I am overwhelmed, I cannot detect it in the client I am trying to help and we are both stuck in the hole. There are many articles and books on how you manage who you are. There are articles, there is the amazing google machine and so you can validate or disprove most things that you see, and you hear, and you are told.

Perhaps the most misrepresented fact is that most clairsentient people are aware that they are clairsentient and the suffering is sadly self-inflicted. We are the largest group of psychically gifted folk and so it is assumed that we know what and who we are. This is quite simply a self-perpetuating myth which has resulted in way too much anxiety and self-doubt, strait jackets and padded cells.

I have another work page. It's how you became a keen observer of the passing parade and discerning that stressful situations do not have to be part of your life. It is incredibly easy to get drawn into other people's calamities and that is when we get overwhelmed. If we are able to step back (the healing journey hard learned) then we allow calmness in our personal space.

What are you feeling right now? Can you express it in words? (or maybe interpretive dance lol).

_____

_____

_____

_____

_____

_____

_____

_____

_____

_____

_____

_____

_____

_____

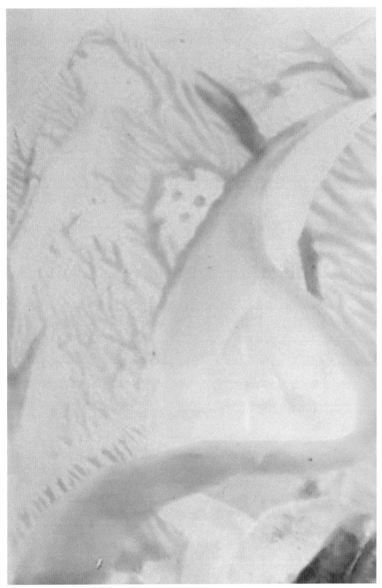

"Light Force" – (Encaustic Wax Art) original by Spider Ward, 2014

Clairsentient abilities allow you to be more accurate. Procrastination ceases to be a life skill and you begin to focus on curiosity. How does this fit into my life, what am I going to do with it, do I share this new found knowledge with the world or do I trust that I will be better for the experience.

The extraordinary thing about clear feeling/intuitiveness is that everyone experiences it in a slightly different way. We recognise it in one another and we tend to have a friend base with similar understandings. What you get from this is freedom, less reactive, it becomes less important to tell your side of the story.

People will notice that you are different in a good way, can't put their finger on it, but in a good way. One of those strange little by products is that you smile more. You are more comfortable in your own skin, you become best friend with your solar plexus (your third chakra) and develop a love for anything orange. You may even, dare I say this, try being a vegetarian, and that's a matter of choice depending on your level of sensitivity and empathy.

_____

_____

_____

_____

_____

_____

_____

_____

_____

_____

_____

_____

_____

_____

_____

_____

_____

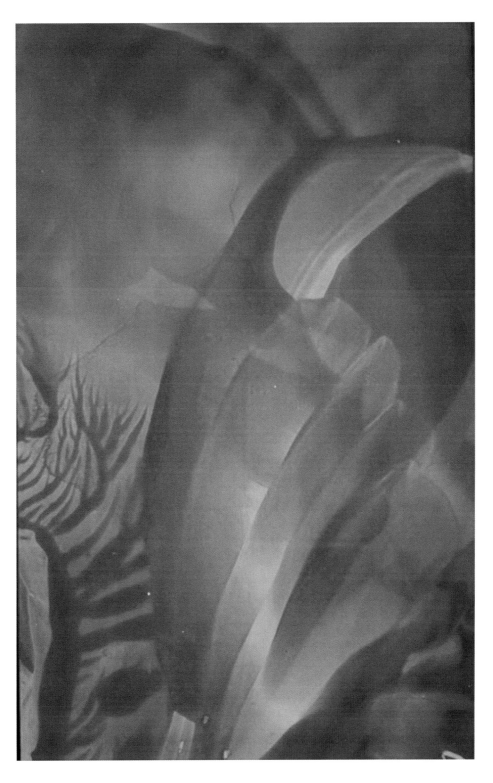

"Follow Passion" – (Encaustic Wax Art) original by Spider Ward, 2014

Clairsentient souls are extraordinarily compassionate and food becomes part of that process. They have a tendency to like root vegetables and comfort food, things like pumpkin soup and homemade bread.

Because they have this extraordinary connection to what we call the "sentient life", if you eat junk you feel like junk. If eating meat makes you suffer and feel drained, don't eat it. There is a wonderful article called "Compassionate Eating" I forget who wrote it but not the essence of the article. When sentient souls eat food that is right for them, they feel more alive, like the light force has been woken up ("it energises us so we can in turn support others"). So when you have a moment, go search.

We have another work page and you're probably getting tired of these, however, you cannot just be clairsentient because I said so, you have to know. So a work page now is a good idea to show you how far you've come and clearly what you are learning, you just write down after a little google search what you have intuitively found.

_____

_____

_____

_____

_____

_____

_____

_____

_____

_____

_____

_____

_____

_____

_____

_____

_____

_____

_____

"Higher Self" – *(Encaustic Wax Art) original by Spider Ward, 2014*

Chakras

The third chakra is the solar-plexus chakra and its colour is yellow, rich and beautiful. Loosely speaking, it's the happy chakra. It's about flow and flexibility. When it is not blocked, it is all about emotions, creativity, sensual pleasure and fantasies and encourages you to feel the world around you. Now, if you went looking for it, then it kind of snugly fits just above your pelvis and your lower belly. It is truly the clairsentient sacred space. Blocked, it shuts down all streams of self-worth and happiness and emotional intimacy and it happens with fear. Fear and anxiety cause malfunction. In sacral chakra can be further aggravated by emotional upset, for example, conflict, loss accident & self-judgment. The way to clear it is not to be afraid, which is a nightmare for the sentient souls who are easily frightened. When your world turns chaotic then we are always certain, in this chaotic place, that we are to blame for the emotional upsets. This is a lesson learnt when we are very young and always comes from an ego based source. Unlearning is a slow process which sooths the confusion and allows understanding and discernment to take place.

Crystals

The ambient treasure for the clairsentient soul is our link with where we came from (our life eons ago), rocks and crystals formed in the earth's core in some cases are as old as our souls and we will be drawn to the comfort, just holding them, or being in their presence. The way of the ancients makes sense to clairsentience; should they get lost in the modern century where we are accused of being too emotional, over emotional, attention seeking and weak!

It has been my practice to choose the stone/crystal and then find out what it is for. The beauty of this is that I actually trust the universe to deliver to me something tangible that I can hold in my hand like citron or amethyst or bronzite or topaz and each time it is my job to find out why I was drawn to the object. At the moment it is lavender quartz which I discovered is about healing and joy. I also discovered that it helps with the lack of self-worth and low self-esteem and it enhances appreciation of the things that are around you. I also discovered it's a type of rose quartz, a bit higher on the pecking order than rose quartz and not as gentle as the unconditional love that abides in rose quartz. My wonderful lavender helps greatly in the healing of the emotional, spiritual self and healing the physical feelings that "I am the victim", and shifts it to something better, nurturing and supporting, caring and compassionate and able to heal mind, body and soul.

Clairsentient Protection Technique

Against the Mortal Enemy (a brief overview)

Spiritual metaphysics is not physical. We, as spiritual metaphysicians, believe that the mind, body and soul/spirit, is a separation of the illusion. Therefore, we have physical knowledge, we have mental knowledge and we have soul knowledge. How we understand the properties of these, is learnt through perception.

So, it is reasonable that we must somewhere in our understanding, acknowledge separation between good and evil, or negative and positive, or light and dark energies.

Dark energetic vibrations are designed to create disturbances in the aura or energetic and physical bodies of a person or place. It is worthy to note that not every bad situation in a person's life is a result of a psychic attack and yet they do happen and problems do happen due to psychic attack in the modern century more than ever before. Heaven and earth are full of more mysteries than we will ever be able to explain. Not everything that goes wrong is due to psychic attack. Psychic attack is very specific in its intention.

While we protect our physical bodies from sunburn and we insure our houses against all sorts of disasters. We are not as vigilant in looking after our souls and complacency has allowed us to find ourselves in abnormal, vulnerable, dangerous situations. That notably causes harm and damage or both, without us really knowing how this happened. A carefully taught belief is that it always happens to someone else, not to us.

This is a Q & A moment with Spider & Spider. Some of this may sound like common sense and some of it may be enlightening. The bottom line is all clairsentient folk have a life purpose challenge and that is to learn discernment.

Discernment is defined as the ability to notice the fine point details, the ability to judge something well or the ability to understand and comprehend something. By noticing the distinctive details in a painting and understanding what makes art good and bad is an example of discernment. (https://yourdictionary.com).

This is a guideline for discerning positive energies. You feel good, you find yourself in safe places, you see joy in God and the creator, and you do not have to ask if this is the truth, you are confident of divine presence. If you are not sure, then you feel comfortable asking, are you of the divine? Are you a loving energy?

This is a guideline for discerning negative energies. You feel fear, and there doesn't seem to be a clear reason. Sometimes tightness in the chest, a sense of foreboding (something bad is going to happen), you become overwhelmed, you don't think clearly and I suppose it's a bit like baby brain or brain fog. When negative energies are impacting, the discernment requires you to know whether or not it is real and therefore you are in danger or it is imagined. Either way "get out now"! Anything that makes us feel uncomfortable, that we can't explain, we must choose to take a step back. When we do this "butterfly's in the stomach settle", good or bad the situation is not meant for us.

I feel like I am in season five of my life and the writers are just making ridiculous shit happen to keep it interesting (Author unknown).

This is your turn again:

What are you feeling at the moment?

_____

_____

_____

_____

_____

_____

_____

_____

_____

_____

_____

_____

_____

_____

_____

_____

_____

_____

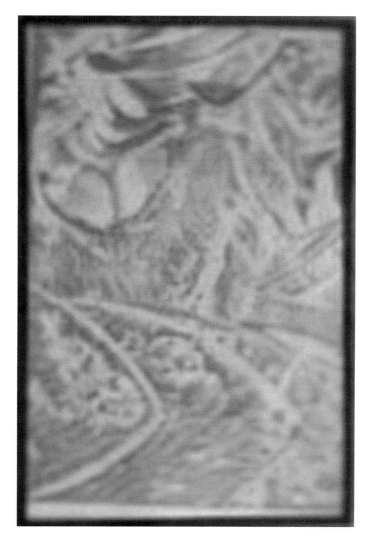

"Angels" – (Encaustic Wax Art) original by Spider Ward, 2014

Psychic Attack

I have taught psychic protection for decades and so I believe that if you insure your car, you insure your house, you should insure your soul. There was last century a school of thought that believed if you left the dark side alone, no harm would come to you. Essentially it sounds like a good idea. However, it's a bit like using weed killer. "The only thing necessary for the triumph of evil is that good men do nothing" (Edmund Burke).

These ideas that I present are because I know who I work for, I work for God, and as a practicing Christian I have found it necessary to walk a path of inclusion and so I draw my faith base from many different spiritual walks of life and hopefully a practical use of common sense. Stuff happens and in life we grow from adversity so if you are frightened in the dark don't just sit there being freighted, get off your ass and turn on the light. I have been working with God for a long time and it has been my experience that if the thought of praying makes you want to throw up, then you are in deep shit and you should give it a try, it is sometimes the only way to clear the darkness. So no I am not requesting everybody to fall on their knees, I am simply saying it works for me. I work with Angels, if I want to work with Angels I have to ask God to send them. It's like he is the CEO. It is the quickest way I know to defeat evil. So if you think you are under attack or you have walked through some evil energy field there are a few things you can do.

As with most clairsentient people, I love affirmations and they pop up on Facebook. The last time I checked I have about 500 in the bank. Wonderful words. So what is an affirmation? "I am safe, I am loved, I am protected at all times", and this is the basis of my belief mantra. I know that I am safe, I know that I am loved and that I am protected. It does not mean I don't get frightened, does not mean I don't get overwhelmed. It means that I have learnt to step back. It means that I have learnt to trust my creator so I can do the work. The hardest thing I had to learn was detachment (not be emotionally invested in the outcome). I have always felt that psychic attacks had a common thread and that was to drain my energy to a point where I can't function. So there are 2 types of psychic attack, one is intentional and one is unintentional a bit like walking through a spider web. So I am now going to talk about negative energies as the bad guys. The bad guy's job is to destroy the good guys this is not rocket science, really it's their only job and so they tend to target weaker human spirits. People who are drug and alcohol effected, someone once said "humans are quite defenceless when they are stoned". So the bad guys are parasites, cleaver parasites and there are lots of ways they can infiltrate your body. My personal sneaky favourite one is, humans enjoying sex, and who would have thought mixing your essence with a bad boy/bad girl would produce absorption of good and bad traits. I am not skipping over how important this protection is, what I expect you to do is research. I expect you to find your own plan. I will give you guidelines, but you need to be aware of what works for you. There are half a dozen methods which help with this, being fully present in the moment, smudging with white sage, black obsidian, onyx, black tourmaline, remember to breathe, cleaning chakra's, rebalancing, include time for meditation. Fill your mind with a song that you know all the words to like, ABBA or Meat Loaf or the big ones Tina Turner. These are but a few. The one to talk about is surrounding yourself with white light, and this, in my experience, is harder for the clairsentient soul to do. In 2008, in a workshop in Singapore, we discovered the pink bubble and that everyone could relate to cotton candy/fairy floss and so each client with their arms outstretched metaphysically built a bubble which we filled with unconditional love with the strength of rose lavender quartz. This allowed the client to immediately feel safe and to breathe and feel grounded. If you are working with the Arch Angel Raphael you may choose a combination of pink and green. This is not because white light doesn't work, it is because clairsentient souls don't have a scent of it where as a clairvoyant soul knows instinctively.

Many of my clients like to do this cleansing as part of their full moon ceremony.

_____

_____

_____

_____

_____

_____

_____

_____

_____

_____

_____

_____

_____

_____

_____

_____

_____

_____

_____

Important

I wasted allot of time in my life desperately wanting my day in court and in this amazing court room everyone who had wronged me was on trial. This need for revenge was my reason for getting out of bed. So deep was the pain that only trial by fire would solve my problems. These mock trials carried on in my head with monotonous regularity, so broken was this damaged child, that it was the only way to function. Wake up with hate, go to bed with hate and, claim the Old Testament revenge "an eye for an eye". In short, in my court, they all had to die!

And then a book called 'The Miracle of Forgiveness' by Spencer W. Kimball and a quote by Maya Angelou.

"There is no greater agony than bearing an untold story inside you" – Maya Angelou.

So learning to forgive "you" after judging yourself for not knowing at any given time what you have done wrong, is the beginning of change. Forgive yourself for who you were in the past, you have changed, you have grown and while you remember her you are not her anymore. But that she was who you needed her to be back then. That she got you to now. And on a regular basis "I forgive Spider for not being the person I want her to be - and I am learning to love her for who she/he/he is becoming".

The greatest protection, the gift we give ourselves, is, not to ignore the truth (regardless of the messenger).

I have discovered a practical truth for those who shoot the messenger. The messenger's job, regardless of who it is, is to deliver the message, your job is to interpret the message, test its validity, and act accordingly. It is of no consequence to you as the receiver of the message to give a shit as to what the messenger thinks about the message. Not the messenger's job. It's a little bit like last century's telegraph boy (a messenger communication sent to or delivered at a telegraph office or post office for transmission by telegraph). https://en.m.wikipedia.org<wiki

The Narcissist and the Empath

There are two groups of people who must be included in this section, the narcissist and the empath.

This is the hottest topic on the radar at the moment and the constant source of fascination. What is it about? This incredibly toxic union that works until it doesn't?

For the narcissist (morally bankrupt and won't change), the empath is the only one who can help her/him. Narcissists are happiest talking about themselves, have complicated fantasies about how amazing they are, truly believing they are the exception to every rule, therefore better than everybody else. This requires constant praise. They also have an arrogant sense of entitlement. They have a charisma that people find attractive and they make great con men. In the blame game they are never wrong.

For the empath, this is what she/he wants, to be needed unconditionally. Sadly it will never be enough. She/he sees the broken, she/he can feel it and now caught in the trap; her mistake is she/he thinks she/he can help because she/he understands.

Before the ink is dry on the contract, in many cases, the empath has become the victim and the whipping boy. Why? She/he stayed too long by the fire.

In order to break free, the empath must acknowledge that they are in an unhealthy and continuously draining relationship. This is a doomed relationship from day one.

The general consensus is the side effects of leaving a toxic relationship. It takes a great deal of courage to cut the ties, you can't be naive, you can't imagine you can still be friends (this is the biggest stumbling block for the empath).

The cut ties must stay cut and the most productive way to try and do this is with a couple of very positive repetitive affirmations.

"I am safe, I am loved, I am protected".

"It's over, he abused me, and I am far away and will never go back".

Should you find yourself a victim of any type of abuse seek help! Generally, that help is actually looking for answers to questions and the coping therapy was not part of the original search. You are not required to explain the narcissist.

As with any relationship that ends, there are feelings of emptiness and grief. I know the feeling.

When you find your voice, I promise it will develop into a compassionate voice who will remind you that you are safe, you are loved, you are protected and you are enough. The slower this process the better the healing. This takes time especially when your only friends are hopelessness and despair.

I have found that I like saying affirmations out loud. They remind me that I have let go of the past.

We must ensure that we are willing to trust our own mind and we have in place personal boundaries. These boundaries need to be achievable, therefore they must be simple to execute. By voicing them out loud we are in fact guarding our boarders. The more you practice, the more you find that you are becoming stronger and more resilient, one step at a time.

Writing will reinforce your positive affirmations to help you cut the ties. Write your own list of self empowering affirmations, to remind you of who you truly are.

_____

_____

_____

_____

_____

_____

_____

_____

_____

_____

_____

_____

_____

_____

_____

_____

_____

_____

"Shadow Dancing" (Encaustic wax art) Original by Spider Ward-Pumfrey 2014.

The Dance

"I will not have you without the darkness that hides within you,

I will not let you have me without the madness that makes me,

If our demons cannot dance, neither can we".

- Nikita Gill

All through this little book of thoughts and solutions – the concurrent theme in them is always choice.

We are all born as unmoulded clay and for me, Carl Jung gave me a sky hook.

Hopefully I am about to give you, the reader, the same thing.

This hook has allowed us to understand some of our complexities. These complexities include righteous indignities, happiness, bliss, peace, rage/anger and I am sure that you could add to these words.

I believe/feel that these complexities help us to create our boundaries. We humans are a wonderful "mosh-pit" of all of these things. Some we share, some we don't. And some we won't.

This is not a chapter on psychology 101 – rather that clairsentient/empaths are truly "beauty and the beast" all rolled up into one neat package. Shadow is called shadow because it's "unwanted"! and part of our life purpose is to accept and integrate. We have choices – and if we choose to integrate this aspect then we are safe, protected and loved or if you like, empowered and able to set boundaries" (not too shabby for something we can't see!). No exceptions/no excuses.

Fighting with self (our own personal demons). Now there is a shift. And we let in the light! It becomes a matter of choice. And based on that choice there is a shift to the light.

There are no guarantees that you will always win and no documentation that you should have to… However, without informed understanding how can we grow and how can we heal?

I suppose the question is do we really want to know the answer? I don't know, but, I do "know the feeling". (do you)?

The whole book is about understanding what I know I feel. So, I guess we have an opportunity together to consider "our options", and our options allow for choice (it must be time for chocolate, or something similar. In fact, it must be time for a lot of chocolate).

These internal monsters (eg. guilt, shame, fear etc.) live with me every day, in fact on a good day I can get 10/10 for breaking the ten commandments before lunch.

We intentionally hide these bloody little monsters. Because nobody in their right mind would make bullets for other judgemental assholes to fire back at us. We like people to think we're kinda' nice and worth knowing.

I have two distinct aspects of my personality "Dolly Do Good" and the "Leviathan Queen" (Satan's only daughter) and I switch them on and off in mid-sentence and they integrate, beautifully.

A sky hook moment is needed (which means feelings need words). Those words come from the "sky hook king", C.G.Jung. Possibly, these words are oversimplified, but in truth...

"We need difficulties, they are necessary for health" – Carl Jung.

Sometimes I choose the Leviathan Queen. She is a warrior who takes no prisoners. In this role I can't be set up, or conned. I don't want to be compassionate I want to be selfish. I don't want to be loved and I certainly don't want to be understanding and forgiving towards anyone who hurts me.

Because….. "I know the feeling"

Then I breath a bit. And my hero Carl Jung, the great (German/Swiss Psychologist and Psychoanalyst) whispers knowingly in my ear.

"There is no lightwork without shadow and no psychic wholeness without imperfection".

(Psychology & Alchemy): this book is Volume 12 in the collected works of C.G. Yung. It is Yung's study of analogies between Christian Dogma and psychical symbolism originally published 1944).

(Warts and all), we are able to take care of our 'person' (ourself) until the cracks appear. We find ourselves painted into a corner where there appears to be only one choice.

However I feel there is probably two choices, each with their own set of consequences.

Some of us have to get to the core/bottom of a problem, and we have to know every single detail from every player in the game and then we have to have the last word. We have to be right! Or we can't solve the problem. My way or the highway.

Anger grows into rage when we quash it (suppress it) for too long. The quash becomes the strength in the shadow, and the shadow is always on stand-by.

"Am I the shadow in the mirror" short answer "No" (shadow self – is very, very simply what I

don't like about me, what I don't want anyone to know exists in me!) Jung gets me and what I see as my flaws. Without the flaws I can't be me, and believe me "I know the feeling".

Where exactly does the shadow fit? We could I suppose give it another name. Let's be dramatic, (the mask). Ironically while I am trying to be honest here with you, I'm wearing my mask, we wear the mask, so people (wherever they are, including myself), will think I am a nice person, not too bad at all.

Imagine we have very clever weapons against ego – we are nothing like a narcissist. We are not toxic, we are the other one, the nice one, and the one that can't lie straight in bed "the great pretender". Shadow is not the pretender. Shadow is the mastermind.

Shadow encompasses everything that we would cast into the black hole of 'oblivion'. When it comes to shadow, ego becomes perfection (see diagram below, figure 5 Jung's Model of the Psyche).

Ego's flaws, according to ego don't exist. Ego always notices the flaws in others, which ego doesn't have (eg. sexuality/preferences, the things we covert, we want what belongs to another). Actually, shadow is anything that we feel guilty about, anything that we are ashamed of in ourselves. Short version – ego is fixed and rigid and shadow is able to bend and recognize all this negative "stuff" and skillfully project it to magically appear in others.

Just like the passage from the Philosophical Tree, page 335.

"When we perceive a moral deficiency in others, we can be sure that there is a similar inferiority within ourselves. "If you feel", Von Franz, writes an overwhelming rage coming up in you - when a friend reproaches you about a fault, you can be fairly sure that you will find your part of her shadow is the bit of which you are delightfully unconscious".

If we choose our resentment towards ourselves and others, if we coincide the moral aspects of our behaviours, then we have the opportunity to bring the shadow into consciousness, and advise a renewal and sense of strength and independence.

Figure 5: Jung's Model of the Psyche.

http://medium.com/personal-growth/4-carl-jung-theories-explained-persona-shadowanima-animus-the-self-4ab6d

It seems to me that all humans are truly a melting pot made up of all sorts of things. In life we all learn how to behave in polite society. The disciplines required to live in society, whatever that may be.

We are encouraged to learn, to share and to be kind, to tell the truth and not to steal etc.

These things include good and bad. "Oversimplified, I hear from the back of the bus" and you are quite right, "I know the feeling I know the feeling" it's part of me. it's part of you, we both know the feeling.

Most of the time we just want to fit somewhere, with someone. Exploring my dark side is supposed to ensure my authenticity. Bullshit! It just makes the mask quicker and easier to put on.

"Well, Clarice, have the lambs stopped screaming" (Hannibal Lecter).

I need me to be the fit. I need to feel the fit. Not what other people think I should be, and to do that I need to understand and respect that I have an enormous capacity to be Hannibal Lecter (the second).

Hannibal's skill lies in double meanings and reasonable doubt a perfect marriage of shadow and ego. (for example, "Killing must feel good to God too….. I do wish we could chat longer but I'm having an old friend for dinner…. discourtesy is unspeakably ugly to me…. without death we would be at a loss"). www.screenrant.com>lists

So, shadows have roots like a plant and shadows prefer to grow in the dark. The more we fear shadows, and discovery by others, the stronger the roots become. The demon becomes incidental when we no longer care what others think. Ego left unchecked and made accountable becomes more unbearable each day. It becomes exhausting and is capable of pushing us into fear. There is probably an argument in defense of ego, however, for the purpose of this discussion, ego can be defeated by knowledge and knowledge dwells in the light and that mercifully is the gift - we always have a choice.

Generally, the only person who has been a witness to my testimony is my shadow. I am never alone, we "manage me" together – neither of us – have to explain, we remember it all

– sometimes even in journaling we don't betray each other – we leave it in the dark. There is peace between us, an understanding. A Trust.

We have now mellowed to a point where we can be kind to each other. Respect grows. The voice of reason becomes "the bugler's last post" and the healing begins.

"If your passion does not include yourself, it is incomplete" (Buddha).

Eventually we all get the opportunity to switch the light on (or not). As sure as night follows day, we will always be faced with choices based on whether the light is on or off.

The soul purpose of the dark is so you can experience light. You get "to see the bullets coming", very hard to dodge a bullet in the dark. Once the light is on, there is only transparency. And if we follow Lord Buddha's teaching then we see this transparency through compassionate eyes.

The simplest explanation

"the shadow is the side of your personality that contains all the parts of yourself that you don't want to admit to having". www.harleytherapy.co.uk<shadow

So here we are, end of another chapter, you know the drill by now.

"Every man carries with him through life a mirror as unique and impossible to get rid of as his shadow" (The Dyer's Hand: W.H. Auden).

We are almost at the end of the book (our book). This is your opportunity to add your words and feelings. We have reached a point together where every person who buys the book, has in fact their own unique copy of the book written with me. A unique version of "I know the feeling" with a running commentary by the reader.

_____

_____

_____

_____

_____

The Last Bit

We have come so far since page one!

We are not so different you and I. There is no sin in caring.

This circle we call life always comes full circle. There comes a moment when you feel your value. There is an obvious shift in your energy levels which is distinctively positive. This positiveness attracts new people who recognise and value your worth. For this to work, you must be the first to recognise it.

How do we achieve this with boundaries?

"Feelers are givers and "givers" need to set limits" because in the real world those who take very rarely give.

I know the feeling.

Thank you for letting me share time on your journey. We all talk about a happy life and I am proof that it is generally achievable. The progress made towards this required me to accept concepts that were alien that "rest, recovery and reflection" were mandatory tools in working towards being empowered. I had to literally "destroy" any ideas that I had to be continually working like a machine in order to win. That somehow if I made myself bullet proof I could beat my demons.

You may have discovered that you are indeed a clairsentient/empath or perhaps you now understand someone who is.

We humans make monumental mistakes, sometimes over and over (because sometimes we are very slow learners, and overwhelmingly stubborn).

When the clairsentient soul answers the call for help without fail they empower the client/friend to hear the things that bring comfort and solution. We know the feeling. We have waited all of our lives for someone to say them to us. The solution here is the lightbulb moment that you are the one and the only one who can tell you, you are loved, you are protected, you are safe.

It is, I feel, inevitable that we eventually grow. We learn that forgiveness isn't so bad; in fact it ushers in a peace which allows us to heal ourselves. Someone once said "you know you have forgiven wrong doing when it has a safe passage through your mind" (unknown).

I think that covers it pretty well. The less airspace you give the people and things that have hurt you, the less your wounds fester, and over time, if allowed, heal. You have not condoned any transgressors you have simply moved on. Like being happy is a choice, so it is with forgiveness, we get to move on. I know you already have things in place that keep you safe (some may be quite automatic and you don't realise you are already doing them).

PS I've just had this great idea. Let's write a book together. Let's collaborate. Let's call it "We Know the Feeling"

If you are getting goosebumps and you want to send me your words from the chapter that turned the light on for you. Pick your chapter from "The Beginning" to "The Last Bit" and claim it now. And Voila, we aren't alone anymore because "We Know the Feeling". You can contact me via my Publisher, Xlibris or Facebook: FabulousFlawsomeSolutions https://www.facebook.com/Fabulous-Flawsome-Solutions-192781861254056

This is not the end, this is the beginning. Empowered, Love, Safe and Protected. Let's keep the light on … just saying.

I feel we can switch the light on for everyone in the dark, who cannot do it for themselves, for those who cannot reach the switch.

If you're not sure, sit in the dark with a torch in your hand and switch it on.

What did you feel between the dark and the light?

For those who can't find the words, We Know the Feeling.

Namaste

Books on Spiders Shelf

These are some of the treasures that can be found at Spiders place:

- The Miracle of Forgiveness by Spencer W Kimble

- The Practitioners Guide to Identify the Mental Health Issues by Dr Liner Amalie

- Crystal's by Rachelle Charman.

- 5 Languages of Love by Gary Chapman

- Being an Empath Kid by Christie Lyons

- The King James Bible

- The Tora

- The Koran

- The Road to Happiness by Delhi Lama

- You Can Heal Your Life by Louise Hay

- How To Overcome Stress Naturally by Tracey Stranger

Spider's Bio

PSYCHIC PROFILING with Spider Ward unlocks all the fear and helps heal by letting go of the past. Choose to be protected at all times on your personal sacred journey! "The best way to avoid problems is to anticipate them". You are made up of physical DNA and spiritual DNA. These two energies are who you are. In these amazing days of change we need honest answers – tough questions with real answers – profiling is a guided session which finds blockages, what's holding you back, what's hurting you and causing you harm. I do not predict the future, there is always your free choice – and you can change your future because it is not yet written. In profiling, I will tell you what you need to know and do to manage any given problem. Most things in this lifetime are not what they seem – profiling lifts the veil – the truth of the situation is there for you and it is my job to help you find it! All profiling is directed by guides and Angels, particularly Arch Angel Michael and ascended guides associated with your situation, especially, your own guides and loved ones.

Spider Ward is a professional psychic profiler and accredited solution based counsellor. She has a natural empathy with clairsentient/claircognizant and clairvoyant gifts, who cares about you! She was involved in metaphysical fields for many years now, and continues studying and writing, travelling and teaching the world.

Spider trained as a nurse at RNSH in Sydney 1972, then in 1987 became a Chef at SANFL Adelaide, teaching and counselling and the learning continued at the University of South Australia. She is certified by Dr. Doreen Virtue PhD. (sometime in January 2017, Doreen had an experience, in which she refuted her new age works. She then become a Born Again Christian, I respect her rights to make the choices best for her).

In 2017, Spider's studies took her to post grad studies in counselling. After graduating she is now an accredited member of the Australian Counselling Association.

Spider is also a member of the International Psychics Association and has been featured in Spheres (The Spirit Guide Magazine). Her public appearances also include television and radio in Malaysia and Singapore. She has also authored the collection of stories ("Spider and Frog").

In 2019, Spider was the recipient of the Psychic Hall of Fame Award by the International Psychics Association.

"Do the best you can until you know better
then, when you know better, do better"
– Maya Angelou.

Printed in the United States
By Bookmasters